A Return to the Heart of Love

First published by sweetspotbooks 2024

Copyright © 2024 by Mary Mallia

All rights reserved. No part of this publication may be reproduced, stored or transmitted in any form or by any means, electronic, mechanical, photocopying, recording, scanning, or otherwise without written permission from the publisher. It is illegal to copy this book, post it to a website, or distribute it by any other means without permission.

This novel is entirely a work of fiction. The names, characters and incidents portrayed in it are the work of the author's imagination. Any resemblance to actual persons, living or dead, events or localities is entirely coincidental.

Mary Mallia asserts the moral right to be identified as the author of this work.

Mary Mallia has no responsibility for the persistence or accuracy of URLs for external or third-party Internet Websites referred to in this publication and does not guarantee that any content on such Websites is, or will remain, accurate or appropriate.

Designations used by companies to distinguish their products are often claimed as trademarks. All brand names and product names used in this book and on its cover are trade names, service marks, trademarks and registered trademarks of their respective owners. The publishers and the book are not associated with any product or vendor mentioned in this book. None of the companies referenced within the book have endorsed the book.

First edition

*This book was professionally typeset on Reedsy.
Find out more at reedsy.com*

*To all pilgrims journeying towards truth, freedom and authenticity
reverberating in sacred Life-Love-Light infinitely -
realizing it is all already there,
in the depths of the heart where
Sacred Spirit and Soul Divine
with heart, mind, body align.*

"The truth shall set you free."

                                    The Christ

Mary Mallia

19/6/2025.

Contents

I Part One

Chapter 1	3
Chapter 2	5
Chapter 3	7
Chapter 4	9
Chapter 5	11
Chapter 6	14
Chapter 7	17
Chapter 8	20
Chapter 9	22
Chapter 10	25
Chapter 11	27
Chapter 12	29

II Part Two

Chapter 13	35
Chapter 14	37
Chapter 15	40
Chapter 16	42
Chapter 17	46
Chapter 18	50

Chapter 19	52
Chapter 20	57
Chapter 21	59
Chapter 22	61
Chapter 23	63
Chapter 24	66

III Part Three

Chapter 25	71
Chapter 26	77
Chapter 27	80
Chapter 28	82
Chapter 29	86
Chapter 30	89
Chapter 31	92
Chapter 32	94
Chapter 33	97
Chapter 34	100
Chapter 35	102
Chapter 36	106

IV Part Four

Chapter 37	111
Chapter 38	114
Chapter 39	117
Chapter 40	120
Chapter 41	122
Chapter 42	124
Chapter 43	127

Chapter 44	129
Chapter 45	132
Chapter 46	134
Chapter 47	136
Chapter 48	138
Chapter 49	142
Chapter 50	143

V APPENDIX

I

Part One

<u>*Heeding the Call - The Call of Love*</u>

*This is the time to go within
in a deep silence free from din.
Through the door of your heart, its music comes
and of a sacred life, love and light it sweetly hums.
You're invited to sit calmly and quietly still
allowing its sweet melody your whole being fill
as when the door opens - this sound like a sunbeam
will illuminate your world - your whole, entire being -
the heavy load lightens
darkness it frightens
fears melt away -
as you come through Love's sacred doorway.*

Chapter 1

The Call of Love

Heed the call of Love summoning from the infinite
　space within.
　Listen intently to its calling as its beating heart
　sings therein,
　of Love's infinite Life, Light, peace and joy,
　as they dance
　to its pulsating rhythm, within and without
　as in a trance.

Skipping ecstatically, celebrating Love's lust for life,
　letting go of all fear, anger and distressing strife;
　allowing it to flow forth freely and trusting it will
　flood your whole being, with its peace so tranquil.

Do not doubt for a minute that this is not so.
　Trust fully in your own soul's ability to glow -
　in its inherent bliss and joy - bringing forth,
　your sundered spirit from west, south, east and north

Bringing bits scattered across the Earth and outer space -
  scraps that had been lost and fallen from grace.
  These suddenly reappear to be made whole,
  graciously uniting mind, body, heart, spirit, soul
  into one complete being, as was always intended
  this unity - on all parts returning, depended,
  Love's true path cleared, lushly resplendent
  with exquisite jewels and a garment of silk,
  a treasure trove whose golden light - its ilk
  is to fill your whole being and that of the Earth,
  vibrations, dimensions expanding giving birth
  to …
  a wholeness whose peace and Life forever abide
  a wholeness whose peace and Love never subside
  a wholeness whose joy wipes away all tears -
  a wholeness whose Light casts out all fears.

And so, for today, take a moment to rest,
  as I graciously invite you this theory to test,
  listening intently to Love's sweet song calling,
  waiting in the shade underneath its cool awning.
  It sings to you of your own divine nature
  dancing its dance in a physical structure,
  your heart will flutter, your body rejoice,
  as Love's calling whispers of unity,
  equanimity
  harmony
  peace
  bliss
  joy.

Chapter 2

The First Step

Walking ahead with our heads held up high
   our own true nature, we embrace not deny.
   Our being's alive, embraced and beheld -
   our power is claimed - nothing's withheld.

Our own true power to be loved, loving, and to love,
   connecting to another with the purity of a dove
   Our own true desire for a fusion that's true,
   comes from deep within me and deep within you.

Seeking outside what lies so latent within.
   looking outside for what lies hidden, therein -
   When we pause in stillness for a moment or two,
   it gleefully comes rushing from within me and you.

It is being set free - from a stuffy space confined,
   this power wants to fly freely, space re-define -
   to soar to new places, new views and new sights,

to sample life's simple, yet delicious delights.

Love's spirit is finally set free to ascend
   on being free from fear, this does depend,
   realising the power that comes from Love,
   that sacred divine power that lifts us above …

All the choas, all the confusing confusion,
   back to Love, free from fear and delusion,
   connected to the essence of our being divine,
   home-ward bound to Love, where all is fine.

Home is not a confined, dark, angry cage,
   stone-cold, fearful, overflowing with rage.
   Home is filled with Life, Love, Light's delight,
   home is where the soul rests after its flight!

Chapter 3

<u>Heeding the Call</u>

Heeding the call of the dawn of being,
   welcoming the day when by your inner seeing,
   your heart opens gently, an opening to the side -
   the door to where sacred Life, Love, Light abide.

The door is ajar, opening fully soon
   overlooking a garden in a bright silver moon.
   The key is ever so slowly turning,
   Love's desire to love – its yearning…

The heart's desire to love and to be loved,
   the aspects of Lover, Loved, Beloved,
   from the beginning of time immortal -
   journeys to the soul's own loving portal.

And through the motions of life's ups
   and downs,
   through ecstatic smiles and
   delusional frowns,

above and beyond all our hopes and
freezing fears -
Love's compassionate blanket dries
away all our tears.

There is no division, rejection or untrue words or deeds,
   sacred Love, the soul of lover and beloved richly feeds.
   "Is this humanly possible ?" some of us may ask,
   "All day and night in the warmth of Love bask?"

Within each and every one of us mere human embodiment,
   lives a force inside so powerful, pure, peaceful, potent -
   not realised for what or who it truly is, or what it can do,
   its underestimated truth and power too -

Lies dormant. Asleep, from deep slumber wants waking up.
   Love's peace and unending bliss fill our golden cup
   to overflowing, throughout our being - everywhere -
   Love's rivers flow abundantly, with oceans to spare.

Chapter 4

<u>Simply Sitting</u>

When life's troubles come to spin you right round,
   let the wearied body rest in Spirit's own sound.
   The sound of the universe speaking to you -
   just listen intently, not much more you can do.

Allow yourself to simply sit, and freshly look,
   (as if your being were a brand-new book)
   at yourself, with a wide open *spacious* seeing,
   perceiving your whole - entire being.
   Not judging the why's or the wherefore's
   of what's coming to be seen. Therefore,
   freely allowing it all to slowly surface -
   this is the crux of this simple practice.

Sitting...
   allowing it all to simply be there,
   free from fear of being laid bare.
   Silently sitting and openly staring,

to upset the ensuing stillness, not daring.
Gazing out into space with eyes softly open,
resting your gaze slowly expanding upon
the space in front, inside and beyond -
Being in the spaciousness of space - fearless -
being here in the now, strength not weakness.

In the midst of thoughts, actions, naming, blaming,
or shaming,
you are not your thoughts, or your mind's
constant gaming.
You are not your words, fantasies or even your thinking -
you'll find your true being springs forth in the twinkling
of an eye, as you suddenly experience the presence -
of what makes you - your own sacred, divine essence.

And after a while of just simply sitting,
observing with a soft spacious gaze
the comings and goings of the busy mind
and its confusing haze -
You come to a point of realising deep inside,
your true essence, which there likes to hide.
Without further ado, with courage and resolve,
allow this essence's pure golden glow to dissolve,
into the depths of your being - inside deep within,
as you continue to sit away from the din -
it continues to spread, permeating your being
and beyond - feel its sacred energy beaming.
Simply rest therein -
glowing without and within.

Chapter 5

<u>Stripped Stark Naked</u>

"But, how do we cope when we feel like life has
   stripped us naked
   and we cannot dance, but want to hide?
   When we cannot leap for joy as we are dying inside?"

Stripped naked with nothing left inside,
   stark naked with nowhere left to hide.
   No shiny silk adorned garments or golden crowns for me,
   Just a plain ache… a pain… a hurt…nothing pleasant to see.

Stripped naked crawling on the dirty, dusty floor,
   stark naked my shining light, seems light no more.
   Darkness covers my legs, my belly, my chest, my face,
   my head.
   There is no light, but fear, and anguish filling my
   being instead.

I slowly fumble along the dark-filled room,

staggering as the dim light is fading soon.
A dark cloud envelopes my whole body and spirit,
I strain my eyes, my ears, and am tested to the limit.

Wherever I turn there is a void and an emptiness,
   wherever I go, I try to see happiness -
   But, like a butterfly fluttering it quickly eludes me,
   leaving my heart, body and bones stripped of glee.

Where do I go from here, what do I do?
   I can't at the mo' be happy like you, you or you!
   My heart shudders, my body trembles and shakes,
   a fear, a sadness, my peace from my being takes.

Just for now, I'll take a deep breath and rest.
   Just for now, I'll be still – this too will pass, this test!
   Just for this moment, I glance at the sky,
   I relish this breath, as I take a deep sigh.

I gaze in the mirror. And what do I see?
   Do I see a beautiful person looking back at me?
   Made in the image and liking of Creator divine?
   My body - my spirit does not define or confine.

So, I look a bit closer with a kind, loving, open heart,
   noticing the warm glow in my chest is about to start
   throbbing. I allow it to e-x-p-a-n-d, filling my body,
   my whole being; my heart this glow does embody.

The warm golden glow in the mirror moves closer to me;
   the warm golden glow in the mirror is what I can see.

CHAPTER 5

It fills and settles into my boundless body, heart, mind, chest,
bringing my whole being suddenly to a place of stillness to rest.

I stand (or sit) there (cross-legged or) with feet wide apart -
   I stand there (or sit) with the warm glow still in my heart
   I stand there (or sit) breathing softly in and out -
   I stand there (or sit) as the glow spreads slowly about.

It's spreading slowly throughout the whole of my being,
   filling each cell with its Love; now my eyes seeing
   not the physical body, but the divine glow within me,
   my true divine nature I freely embrace and embody.

Chapter 6

The Test

When it's like the beaten track is wearing you down
    and all you want to do is up and leave town,
    just take a minute to breathe, rest and repose -
    until the time comes for the test to pass - I suppose.

The test is not always a salient simple task.
    Sometimes it seems like you're wearing a mask
    of smiling, chirping, dancing and thinking,
    whilst deep down inside your heart is sinking.

At times like this, your bright white healing light,
    wants to shine forth, it wants to beam bright -
    the whole of your being it longs to fill
    with its bliss, joy and peace so tranquil.

Now pause for a moment and silently still be -
    until it expands throughout your whole being.
    There is nothing to think, analyse, judge or do,

just being with how things are - just be you.

As you begin to rest in Light's warm soft embrace
   your whole being begins to feel full of grace.
   The Light of Consciousness, sacred and divine -
   flows forth, you and your world to newly define.

It sustains your whole existence today and always,
   protects through life's dark dangerous alleyways -
   It lights up many a dark dusty deserted street,
   in which no kindred spirit you are likely to meet.

And yet, as you rest in the comfort of Light's warm
   gentle glow -
   a luminescence shines through each and every row
   of houses, in the here and the now as you walk,
   with your warm golden glow within, you talk
   of loves lost and of loves that have been found -
   of labels, names, games that the mind confound,
   of dark, dreary days when you seem to forget -
   the warm golden glow within is already there! Set ...

To guide with its wisdom and conscious light,
   waking your soul up to shine ever so bright.
   It reminds you of what lays hidden out of sight,
   ready to forge forth with power and might ...

With kindness, compassion, patience and wisdom,
   Light within us establishes its luminous kingdom,
   putting all our wrongs, right - setting all straight -
   Our pasts, our futures, our present, as we patiently wait ...

For its bright silver ray and warm golden glow to beam,
 filling mind, body and soul to the brim, it does seem
 to fill the depths of our hearts with contentment
 and with a bliss, peace, joy, equanimity opulent.

And when this union so pure, so divine -
 this union within, in which everything's fine,
 where there is no past or future about which to worry,
 there our souls rests in a peaceful equanimity.

Chapter 7

<u>The Struggle</u>

It is a most sacred Love divine -
   wanting to embrace this heart of mine.
   A pure love with no limits or boundaries,
   expanding across nations, entire populations.

The biggest challenge and my only offense,
   a cold-stone fort constructed as my defense.
   I mock divine Love and its sacred plan:
   "Come on, come in - only if you can!"

Love replies, in a sad sort of way,
   as my bricks and mortar seem there to stay:
   "I cannot come in, if you block me out.
   Your taunting words, I hear you shout."

<u>My Soul's Reply:</u>

"I'm so scared to let you in,
   amidst my chaos and din.

I'm ashamed of my state of affairs,
and anyway, in my life nobody cares.
I walk alone, abandoned, dejected,
the laws of Love having rejected.
There's nobody out there for me,
I walk all alone, as you can see.
I take pride in stumbling, weak upon the ground
waiting for when the next fall will come around.
It doesn't occur to me there may be another way,
although I have heard and have known others say
that the Christ has come, a new way of life teaching,
for humankind harmony, unity and peace reaching.
I can see my ways have been terribly skewed,
My being's trampled upon, it needs renewed.

Alas, as I fall
   for help I call
   but nobody's around
   to hear the sound -
   of my voiceless anguished pain.
   Writhing inside, in agony again and again,
   not that I want to whinge or complain
   but, this life I can't any longer sustain,
   in this state of being, I cannot remain.
   Yet, what to do? Where to go?
   I'm waking up, please let me know."

Love's Reply:

"Go the the centre of your heart - there,
   in fullness and sweetness is where -

CHAPTER 7

My Love sings within you its jubilant muse.
Stop what you're doing and put on your shoes!
Let's undertake the longest journey so far -
the one from your busy mind to your illumined heart.
There is no past or fearfully frightening future to dread,
just the warmth of my Love on the path you now tread."

Chapter 8

<u>The Voice of Love Speaks</u>

In front of the mirror you sit or stand tall -
   In front of the mirror you feel great, big, little or small.
   Close your eyes momentarily for the image you see,
   is not out there on the wall - but inside you and me.

Tread gently and carefully, go softly and with care,
   for agitation, the still presence inside is likely to scare -
   in the chest part of the body where the heart lives inside,
   a soft silvery light and warm golden glow silently abide.

Amidst all the labels, the blames and the manipulative games
   Amongst all the judging, the fears, the names, the shames,
   deeply hidden in the imperceptible recesses of every heart
   lies a silent Life and Light all enveloped in Love.

The Love within whispers quietly: "Do not be afraid -
   come in a bit closer - it's OK - it's OK.
   I've been waiting ardently for the day you would come,

CHAPTER 8

I'm ever so joyfully ever-present, your welcome's begun.

I welcome you profusely to the Source of your very own being,
   to the place accessible only through your eyes' inner seeing.
   I do not judge through names, labels, guilt, anger or fear,
   you're welcome through the unconditional Love that is here

   Never a word or thought of judgement or shame,
   never daring or wanting to point a finger or blame.

I have sat and waited longing for you to come home to me.
   Your return fills the heavens with a jubilant glee.
   I ask no questions like why, what, where or how?
   I just take you as you are, in the here and in the now."

And just as we have simply been lying down, sitting or standing …
   Gently letting go of all the unnecessary din, understanding
   that this warm cosy golden glow of Love lying within,
   is, has, and will always be silently beating therein.

For a few moments each day to which towards it we draw
   our busy attention, which is busy no more,
   quietly resting in its warmth, peaceful stillness -
   our body's repose,
   our souls' yearning,
   our own mind's willingness.

Chapter 9

<u>The Transformation</u>

When anguished pain comes up, a numb ache deep inside -
   when feelings of dread, greeting each morning abide -
   when the fear of the future pertinent or seemingly true,
   the fear of something void of its own being - untrue ...

A freezing fear that can weaken both body and spirit
   a daunting dread that our life chances does limit -
   a fear so grotesque, so monstrous, so perverse,
   it seems to cripple our whole universe.

The heart shuts down to love and to trust -
   a veil of mistrust over the heart it does thrust,
   numbing the heart's rhythm, silencing its beat,
   making all successes seem more like defeat.

In the ensuing confusion, anger, and crippling fear
   the silvery golden glow inside doesn't seem near -
   covered so aptly with a dusty silk veil,

CHAPTER 9

kept in place with an oxidised old nail

The bright silvery light and warm golden glow inside,
   want to shine outwards from where they reside,
   but blocked by the veil and covered in dust,
   the golden glow seems much more like rust.

Suddenly the veil moves. The dust gently rises -
   the whole of our being confused by surprises,
   is shocked to the core at this movement, it does shudder -
   it doesn't want any more movement. When then another
   shift moves the veil slowly, ever so slightly,
   the veil and the dust move ever so lightly,
   sliding softly to the side ... further to the side ...
   some light shines through the gap created inside.

Through the gap in the veil shines the warm golden glow
   with the silvery white light together bright they flow -
   lighting up the whole of the chest, the back and beyond
   all the dust disappears in a split second.
   The veil continues to slip through the hole,
   it slides and slithers away from the soul -
   unblocking the light, uncovering the glow,
   freedom at last from the dust and the veil. So,
   unexpectedly, yet joyfully, and graciously greeted,
   together mind, body, soul and spirit are seated
   once more in the heart where this unity is greeted.
   In the heart is the essence of all Life-Love-Light,
   filling your being with a snow-white delight.

Pause in this space for a while and take rest -
feel what's going on, in your heart, in your chest

To experience with your own awareness and mind,
  that which within the body and the heart does abide.
  An essence golden, silver and white so sublime,
  rest your gaze, have a look, an experience divine ...

Of what lies beyond the names, the labels and the fears -
  of what lies beyond conditioning, brain-washing and tears ...
  of what cannot properly by human words be described ...
  can only be felt through an open heart and willing mind.

Allow your awareness and consciousness to rest,
  open, trusting and spacious, this theory to test.
  Do not take what I say as being totally true,
  experience it directly for you ... yes, for you.

Chapter 10

<u>Dancing for Joy</u>

I hope you took some time to rest in a quiet, still place,
   feeling all loved up, full of sacred grace in this space -
   your battered body and weary soul seeming
   to rest in a luminous warm glow gleaming.

Allowing the eyes... the ears... the jaw and the body to soften,
   a sense of spaciousness, of Life-Love-Light will very often
   pervade our Consciousness ...heart... body ...mind ... Spirit,
   as through the softness and ease they are enabled to visit.

The radiance of silvery rays intermingled with gold
   in the chest - the heart centre, their silent abode -
   enliven the heart resting in this loving embrace,
   heaven and earth interlace in this sacred space.

A child-like state of innocence and peace too,
   begins to slowly take hold of me and of you.
   The heart is healed - the damage reversed -

for joy, with rupture the heart's being burst.

This embodied Spirit is now being set free -
   radiating a golden gleam, there within me -
   Not a beauty that fades, nor a body that dies,
   but a soul full of Love, defying space as it flies
   out through your being as free as a bird,
   silently soaring without any word -
   filling your body, heart, soul and mind,
   with a loving peace and joy you will find.

I humbly invite you to engage with this practice,
   wherever you are, whatever your office.
   Mind, body, soul and Spirit come together within,
   freeing the heart previously held captive to sin.
   Dancing swiftly, swirling and gleefully playing,
   your soul, to its true life-path assiduously staying.
   Sacred Love, in the distance, your footsteps can hear -
   waiting for you to enter your heart, loud and clear.
   The exquisite divine dance of your journey's begun,
   now let's all join in within and let's have some fun!

Chapter 11

<u>When She Calls, She Calls</u>

Today as I walked I heard the sound of the land,
   through mud and rocks and shale and sand.
   I looked around, as the musical sound
   its way to my eager ears found.

She beckoned me to her closer get,
   and to never, what lies in my heart, forget.
   She urged me to climb up further along
   from which spot, I heard this sweet song:

"Come to me darling, come to me sweet,
   loosen your tongue and quicken your feet.
   I've awaited your coming for so long,
   come to me darling and join in my song."

Up the hill I hastened, quickening my pace.
   A sense of urgency, pushed me up in haste.
   I clambered and climbed up to the very top,

I'd climbed up far enough, I could now stop.

There on the summit on top of the Tor,
   a voice came a-calling from the sweet portal's door.
   I listened intently as the wind whistled so
   and the song, it continued, it continued to go:

"Come to me darling, come to me sweet,
   loosen your tongue and quicken your feet.
   I've awaited your coming, oh, for so long,
   come to me darling and join in my song."

On top of the Tor, on the side somewhat steep,
   her song softly whispered for my feet to leap
   and boldly go through that sweet portal door,
   to go through trusting, in faith - I shan't fall.

The portal door opened and lo and behold!
   Visions of beauty exquisite like the days of old,
   when as a young maiden, an angel did me visit
   and in a heavenly voice sang songs so exquisite:

"Come to me darling, come to me sweet,
   loosen your tongue and quicken your feet.
   We've all awaited your coming, oh, for so long,
   come in our dearest, and join in our song."

Chapter 12

The Meeting

The Meeting takes place underneath an awning. I invite you to allow yourself to be transported to the most exquisitely peaceful place where the awning or canopy might be placed. Allow your imagination to rest there ... amidst waterfalls, lush vegetation, delicious sunsets or sunrises, on sandy beaches or on green grassy hills – paint your own picture - the sky's the limit. And then in peace and at ease, rest within it.

"Dearly beloved body you have heeded my call,
  dearly beloved heart you are weary no more.
  Dearly beloved soul you have been set free,
  dearly beloved mind, you can now clearly see ...

The indisputable Essence of what you truly are -
  beyond all labels, names, shames, albeit quite bizarre,
  lies a Love full of Life and a Light so sublime,
  a gracious compassion - an experience divine.

Allowing your body in this state of being to rest,
   connecting to the Sacred within you with zest -
   no past or future to worry about or fret,
   just resting in peace is true resting, I bet!"

Lounging in the warm sunshine of Love's pure abode,
   nonchalantly wandering up and down its true road -
   an exciting adventure is about to begin as you meet
   like-minded souls, up and down every street.

They too, like you have heard sacred Love calling -
   They too, like you, have rested in the shade of its awning.
   They too, like you, have danced to its rhythm and beat -
   They too, like you, wander with a heartbeat in the soles
   of their feet!

As you walk ahead , you are pleasantly surprised and glad
   that you too, have opened your ears and clearly heard
   the soothing lullaby of Love's gently whispered song,
   and that you too are now joyfully singing along.

"We are all so pleasantly surprised and in awe when
   the joys of Love unite us. We are all one, then.
   There is no you and I, or me and you -
   there is only Love, with nothing to do.

So come rest in My awning, all gathered as one.
   Just lie in the shade, as your journey's begun -
   The warmth from the sun makes the heart shine so
   bright,
   Love within shines forth – a luminous light."

CHAPTER 12

All others, under the awning with you can feel,
   the soft warm Love within glowing so genteel -
   filling each and everyone with its warm soft beam,
   filling each one with Life and Light in their Being."

II

Part Two

A Return to the Heart of Love

*And so the sweet maiden goes,
caution to the wind, she throws.
Back to Love's tender heart,
of which you, dear reader, are also a part.
On this journey, you're cordially invited to join her
She'll gently, yet firmly, guide you on your way there.*

*"Ahead I go forth, trust I must -
That God's plan, albeit hard, will unfold and work out
for my highest good, and the highest good of all of humanity,
as it realises its divinity and regains its dignity."*

Chapter 13

<u>A Return to Love</u>

I am and have been restored
   in body, mind and Spirit -
   Love joyously comes to visit,
   filling my being with its radiant grace,
   shining through my body, my face.
   Reminding me of my nature, true -
   Divine.
   It's not just me, it's also you.

A new Earth comes
   heralded by drums,
   its birth has begun
   in this time-span.
   The head's crowning, legs spread astride wide,
   fear and fear of death this new birth puts aside.
   A new higher vibration, this heaven on earth,
   and all of creation, joyfully welcomes its birth.

The pure of heart, humbly renew within-
free from fear, anger, guilt, shame or sin.
The clothes they wear, as white as snow,
by sacred Love enveloped. This they know:
a Love so deep and so all-embracing,
a Love that seeps deep into each cell, interlacing
and procuring wholeness, healing, peace and joy,
an equanimity, a harmony for each to enjoy.

The new Earth is now and it is here -
Be compassion, peace, joy – denounce fear.
Allow your whole being to be embraced,
by Life's beauteous sweetness graced.
Allow your whole being to be restored,
in the heavenly realms your soul adored,
to be welcomed back with a great feast,
a celebration, a party -
dancing to the music,
swaying to its beat
eating delicious
morsels sweet.
Spinning around,
to the joyous sound,
of Love freely flowing,
Life's inner knowing
dizzy with delight -
your Light shining bright.

Chapter 14

<u>Here I Come</u>

My ministry's begun.
   Please, please follow The Son.
   Humanity he comes to restore -
   an invite for everyone, forevermore
   to open your eyes to the power of Light,
   how the darkest of darkness it can blight.

Allow your whole Being to heed his message
   open your heart as a rite of passage -
   to a Love which like a madness
   fills your being with a gladness
   knowing no limits, no boundaries -
   no borders, no counties or countries.

But, that most precious human soul,
   to touch it with his word - his goal.
   His word wakes up what is sleeping inside,
   bringing it slowly, yet surely, back to life.

Your Christ-light awakened, ecstatically dances,
your vibration and manifestation, it enhances.

Allow the Christ-light within
to free you from sin,
so that free inside
in him, you'll abide,
as he abides in you,
making the two
united as One -
your soul and The Son.

Christ knows your heart,
as of its true nature a part -
Your ups and your downs,
your smiles, your frowns,
your weakness, your strengths
and to great lengths He will go,
your divine Light to you show.

A divine drizzle of grace tenderly trickles down,
refreshing your whole being through the crown.
That sin which bleeds like scarlet red -
it turns into white snow instead.
Forgiving all that had taken place,
restoring all with a divine gracious grace.
Its presence only in the here – in this moment,
Its nature compassionate, kind, forgiving, clement.
Divine Love abundant constant ever-lasting -
beyond concepts can convey,

or any words, can ever say.

A love so pure, so intense, so deep
  into the depths of your Being it'll seep,
  making you whole, not broken any more
  your spirit into the heavenly realm soar.

Whenever plagued by doubt, anguish or fear -
  allow your Christ-light to shine crystal clear.
  The power of its brilliance underestimated it is,
  transforming into light, the darkest abyss.

So, put your trust in his word -
  know your divine sacred worth.
  His words empower therein
  and set us all free from sin.
  It will set you free,
  able to be -
  the truest version of yourself
  experiencing your true worth.

Take all of this ever so lightly,
  and test it ever so blithely
  practice with confidence,
  examine with diligence.

Be ever so ready,
  quick and steady,
  to make this journey your own.
  The Truth sets you free
  your truest divine self to be.

Chapter 15

<u>The Mother's Yes</u>

I shall forge straight ahead,
   Nada buzzing in my head.
   In me instil
   your divine will,
   and your sacred grace
   At a rapid pace, (please!)
   Acknowledge - me see,
   give me the courage to be
   the mother, breaking free,
   the Mary she's meant to be.
   Send your Spirit divine
   sacred Love sublime
   filling her to the brim
   without and within.

I perceive clearly the power of evil,
   the destructive strength of the devil.*
   Yet, I know you are more strong,
   with You in me, I can't go wrong.

CHAPTER 15

Fully protected by the Nada sound,
Its empowering strength newly-found.
Although with me since the age of six or before,
I now realise its true value and power much more.

Defeating with the mighty pen *The Lord of Illusion*
   killing, with my writing, his deadly delusion.
Restoring Your reign to our parched Earth
people rejoicing, hearts bursting with mirth.
Souls singing at the top of their voices,
as their bodies, Spirits and mind rejoices
at your ultimate victory, which in the end,
a broken humanity comes forth to mend.
Your sacred Spirit fills every one,
not only the Mother and the Son,
upon Its silent transformative descent,
our beings enlightened, begin to ascend.

* The devil in this context relates to any entity of this dimension or any other, which breaks the Law of Love. It throws the Perfect Cosmic Order into chaos, fear, anger and disconnection, which causes suffering , anguish and pain. We are created to live in peace, unity, joy and harmony within the perfection of the Law of Love.

Chapter 16

The Journey Must Go On

Continue to trust in what you are,
   in Love's heart a sacred star
   which shines ever so bright,
   filling all with great delight.
   All bask in Its radiance,
   as you rest in Its presence.

Continue to walk your path, albeit alone,
   trudging along, dodging every stone -
   that in your path may lay,
   an arduous journey waylay.
   Keep walking ahead straight and tall,
   even when trouble knocks at your door.

For you are protected -
   your limbs injected
   with a powerful strength
   taking you to any length,
   to go wherever you need to go

this you must trust and know.
You shall not hurt your feet,
and evil, ye, shall not defeat!

The path you shall have to walk,
   and the speech you shall have to talk,
   shall all be divinely inspired -
   an open heart and mind required,
   connected to the sacred mystery,
   as you fulfill your divine destiny.

Do not be afraid – do not fret,
   don't splash into a puddle and get wet!
   Don't get your knickers in a twist,
   or do something silly like break a wrist
   or marry a millionaire materialist -
   or give into a temptation you can't resist.
   Stay calm and still, collected and cool,
   knowing yourself –your unmatched tool.

And if they want to shut you down
   and politely ask you to leave town,
   then say to them in no uncertain terms:
   "I shall not go, you slimy worms.
   I am here on a sacred mission,
   to fulfill my divine commission
   and leave this town, I shall not,
   be it cold, or be it hot!
   Whether you like me, whether you don't
   leave this town, I definitely won't!"

Confuddled at your newfound power,
   they - your feisty soul seek to devour.
   Your message they also strive to hide,
   with comments unkind sarcastic snide.

Do not be afraid - do not fret,
   don't splash into a puddle and get wet!
   Just don't forget what you are,
   a luminous, dazzling, divine star
   in the heart of God's essence abiding,
   in sacred Life-Love-Light residing.

Your divine commission is coming soon.
   Listen carefully. One sultry afternoon -
   as you bask in the sun's warm embrace,
   overflowing with Love's abundant grace
   you shall be summoned – hear the call,
   to guide humankind, after thelong fall,
   back to their original state -
   before it's all a bit too late.

Get your feet ready
   your legs steady
   to walk the walk
   talk the talk
   travel far -
   by bus, by car
   spill the beans
   of divine kings and queens
   waiting to welcome us all,
   as we hurriedly heed the call.

CHAPTER 16

Hastening to their sacred palace,
   I pray, do not be embarrassed
   to party till the small hours
   in their gardens rich with flowers.
   Or taking a walk by the waterfall,
   or eating delicatessen in the hall,
   raising a crystal glass or two -
   one for me and one for you!

This invitation, the good news is – is open to all -
   Just heed the call, heed the call, heed the call …
   Pack your suitcase
   just in case -
   you have to travel far.
   Or perhaps it's perfect, just where you are.
   Either way, be prepared to hear,
   the divine message loud and clear,
   albeit whispered softly by the breeze
   asking you fear and doubt to release
   so that to the party you may go -
   thoroughly enjoying this life-changing show.

Chapter 17

<u>The Saga</u>

A long unending saga of torture and pain,
   left everybody changed, never the same.
   Hearts alive - died -
   beyond limits tried.
   Love lived amid,
   where life had hid -
   Anguish, dissolved,
   agony, resolved -
   For a heart
   full of grief
   comes relief.

Alas, that bloody murder and death!
   Glorified by some,
   killed also his mum.
   After three days his Being's restored,
   to the heavens uplifted, joyfully adored.
   The anguished pain did silently seep
   into the wooden slabs which did weep

for the evil that took hold of that day
determined to destroy the Son of God,
come what may.

He suffered so much over the years -
   sad morning and night-filled tears
   over souls which were lost, hearts
   of hard cold cobalt, and steel darts
   spearing through his heart to its core.
   Will they know Life and Love anymore?

He looks at them lovingly and
   compassionately
   showers them with peace,
   love and mercy,
   quenching their inner thirst
   until their angry heart burst -
   asking them to come back home to his
   gentle loving heart,
   so that of his and his Father's eternal
   love, they're always a part.

But sadly, they turned their hearts away.
   Nothing their allegiance to the beast could
   sway.
   They had vouched their hearts wholly to him,
   everyday acting out a brand new sin.
   All the time rejecting sacred Light,
   shunning Love, and what is right.
   It saddened the Son -
   and also his mum,

that all that agony and pain,
may have even been in vain.

Humanity's heart had closed,
its soul's light darkened, love deposed.
Locked in its own airless prison cell,
creating a fearful dark frightening hell.
Rejecting The Christ and his way of life,
liberation from slavery, fear, ego, strife.

The freedom which he came to bring,
its knell heralding freedom ringing
in the hearts of those who love the Son,
although he'd hoped it'll be everyone.
They sang of his glory day and night
gathering crowds - a glorious sight.
They would shout out from the top of the hills,
their voices booming through doors and window sills.
For no amount of evil kills
their love for him, their whole heart fills.
They come to the Son, they come to him
with their empty cups, now overflowing -
their eyes and faces presently a-glowing
with Life-Love-Light's gentle loving grace,
pouring abundantly over the human race.

Now his own all welcome him back.
In their hearts abundant Life, no lack
of peace, love, joy as his luminous light
in their hearts and beyond shines bright.

CHAPTER 17

He comes his own to gather and be
with his beloveds, through eternity.

Chapter 18

The Peaceful Way

They rejected him on that fateful day,
   as determined they were, come what may
   to do away with the Son of Man,
   mutilate and murder if they can.

The fateful fall of the whole generation,
   back from every region and every nation,
   sadly let their Creator down, big time -
   His Son they murdered, a legal crime.
   He was passed-over to his foe,
   a brutal death, he would know.

The nation that Abraham and Sarah propagated,
   on that day was relegated
   down into the pits of hell -
   their soul to evil sell.

The whole of the heavens shuddered in fear.
   Mother Mary, The Magdalene and John stayed near
   the Son of God, as he was condemned

CHAPTER 18

and why, they could not comprehend!
How this nation, who since a child had been nursed,
the Son of the hand that fed them in the desert, cursed.
Betrayed through lies, jealousy and deceit,
of death they drummed a dreadful drumbeat,
accusing him of treachery
as he fulfilled his ministry,
gifting to all those who came
the blind, the dumb, the sick, the lame -
a cure, their whole being healed,
in Creator's heart of love sealed.

He taught them The Peaceful Way,
   so that they too, would one day
   work miracles the same as he -
   move mountains, walk across the sea.

But, alas the ending went all sour -
   The Father's most precious sacred flower,
   met a brutal end - murdered - on a cross laid,
   the legacy of this killing with us has stayed.
   And yet, this Son divine, dead did not stay -
   resurrect in him, we shall all one day.

Chapter 19

<u>The Light of Consciousness</u>

Acknowledge, embrace, proclaim the Light.
   May this light divine shine ever so bright.
   Do not stop it - but, keep it lit,
   enlightening the world, bit by bit.

If for some it shines too bright,
   and they cannot bear its light
   then let them gently walk away -
   a way away - let them stay.

For some others, it lightens up a byway -
   or perhaps a previously hidden alleyway,
   that they themselves would love to take.
   But, due to insecurity or fears make
   a judgement call -
   once and for all,
   to stay on the familiar beaten track,
   instead of going forwards, going back.

CHAPTER 19

Your light reminds them of their fall,
 of where they had once been before.
 They are momentarily blinded,
 their life's route re-winded.
 Suddenly stepping back
 to where it's pitch black!
 Where hither 'n' thither,
 hearts whither
 souls darken
 Spirits die.
 In that place
 there is no light
 in sight
 shining bright.

The darkness, a veil of black lace -
 envelopes their deepest, darkest space.
 Your light disturbs this darkened deep pit
 which is full of fear. They sometimes sit
 wondering why your light them annoys,
 in a world full of fear - distracting noise.

They want to clamber back to the light,
 dispel their darkness, and it fight,
 until it's gone and overcome –
 this might be the story for some.

Alas, for some others, the dark stays black –
 they watch the aftermath of their own
 shipwreck.
  Their ship's sturdy sides burst and crushed,

dark engulfing waters, suddenly in rushed
sinking their ship deep -
drowning souls weep.
It's not much fun
on the ocean floor,
where light, is light no more!

Is it too late, or are they in time,
   is the eleventh hour, still yet to chime?
   Will they get out and themselves save,
   or will their souls be swamped by waves
   which their whole being seek to enslave?
   Will they return safely to the top,
   and themselves back to upright prop?
   Will they make it back to the light
   if up they paddle, with all their might?
   Or is it too late, are they not in time,
   is it the twelfth hour's time to chime?

Look and listen at every sign,
   By Life's grace and grand design.
   A message loud - a message clear:
   "The End Of Time approaching - near -
   have no fear, have no fear, have no fear."

Just paddle back up to the top,
   with power, strength and will – Do not stop.
   Go back to the time of innocent childhood
   when carefree faith and trust would
   lift you up, not take you down;
   make you smile, not frown.

CHAPTER 19

You are still in time-
   For the twelfth chime's
   Not gone, yet –
   You can make it, I bet!

Get to the shore and slowly recover
   your breath and gently rediscover
   as you stop and on the sand pause -
   in the here and now, not in what was.
   In the here and now is the grace
   which will sweetly end the phase
   of going back and going forth -
   that place of darkness, toward.

In the here and now is breath
   In the here and now is life
   In the here and now is peace
   In the here and now is bliss
   In the here and now is joy
   In the here and now is life
   In the here and now is love
   In the here and now is light
   In the here and now is infinity
   In the here and now is eternity.

Come, rest and sit.
   It's all well lit
   in the present
   of the Presence -
   in Love's embrace,
   full of divine grace.

In this truth
in your being,
rest tranquil
and sit still -
rest,
realise …

God's waiting -
   Love's gracing
   your way back.
   Despite the crash,
   despite the dark,
   in spite of the din -
   despite drowning –
   He'll take you back. Go!
   He'll take you back, so
   together with Him you shall live,
   His sacred Life, to you, He'll give.
   In sacred love and grace …
   moving
   resting
   breathing
   being.

Chapter 20

Love's Reassuring Whispers

My heart aches as I leave my sons at home,
   to heed the call of the Isle of Avalon.
   Let me, let go of my attachment to them,
   to set them free, as I did You back then,
   to let Love have the fruit of my womb
   whether in a stable, a house or a tomb.
   God resurrects the fruit of my loins,
   back to Him, He gathers my boys.
   He loves how freely I give and offer up His own -
   surrendering our whole being, down to the bone!
   For myself, the grace of God and His favour suffices,
   showing His love for me through His own devices.

I know His blissful peace in my heart.
   What shall I say, where do I start?
   The peace He gives is subtle and sweet,
   where Life-Love-Light in unison meet.
   He blesses me with his divine Spirit,

fills me with His grace beyond limit -
for His love for me and for us all,
I leave everything. I heed the Call.

"Do not dawdle, please get going,
  there His Son the way is showing.
  Don't waste time on looking back,
  walk briskly, forge straight ahead.
  He's the way to be walked,
  He's the word to be talked.
  He's here in you.
  Are you present too?

He'll whisper sweet nothings of Love in your ear
  continuously his sweet music in your ear, you'll hear.
  You'll feel his presence strengthen your bones,
  his power and his strength heighten the tones
  of the sweet inner music playing on your heart-strings,
  sweetly, softly, subtly his sacred Love sings.

Alas, let go of all you attach to -
  walking the way, as you choose to do.
  Be fearless, shameless, pure and true
  and love Him dearly as He loves you!"

Chapter 21

<u>Surrendering</u>

May your sacred will be done in me,
   for your glory all the Earth to see.
   As you have saved your mum -
   You've come to save everyone.

So that free from anguish, pain and fear,
   love, peace and joy can abide here -
   through your beloved people of Light,
   always with your law of Love in sight.
   Shining your sweet Love so pure and true,
   their hearts, minds, bodies, souls renew.
   The heavens on a new earth abound,
   Listen carefully. Ssshh!
   Can you hear its sound?
   Springing forth within each light-worker,
   each humble and authentic life-searcher.
   Truth divine and justice restored,
   sacred Life-Love-Light adored.
   A new creation starting afresh,

free from greed, not ruled by cash.
Love its brand new currency
Light as a matter of urgency
Life according to Creator's sweet plan -
it's how they'll live, God's renewed clan.
His community, His people, His authentic ones,
they start again – children, dads and mums
living on the Earth secure -
fear of death, not anymore!
Bliss in their hearts and joy on the land,
in soil and seed - in every grain of sand.

Chapter 22

The Presence

When demons wage their deadly war on you -
   as they're presently often prone to do
   don't get despondent and don't feel sad
   don't allow yourself to feel beaten or bad.

They come to tempt and lure in the pure,
   their peace and light for themselves procure.
   Securing respite, claiming the light as their own,
   for the darkness which they have sown
   envelopes their whole entire being -
   for the darkest of the darkness is what they sow,
   and the darkness of the darkest is what they know.

When beings of Light
   shine bright -
   the dark ones come to prowl
   with their fangs slimy scowl
   sowing fear, anger, pain -
   seeking the light-beings' light to gain.

The pure light-beings are unaffected.
True to their truth and heart they stay,
keeping the darkest darkness at bay.

Did you know, that the purer the soul does shine,
   with Love sublime and Light divine,
   the more the darkness does fiercely attack
   to take their light and peace? For their lack
   of light, peace and love is maddening,
   their state of being sorely saddening.

So when they whisper words of fear,
   doubt, shame, condemnation, my dear,
   know that I am always here -
   your pleas for help, I do hear.
   My presence strengthens and enlivens
   your own sacred spark of Light divine.

Chapter 23

<u>The Calming of the Storm</u>

A terrible storm rages outside
   shattering my peace, I must confide.
A cruel wind howls through the trees,
   it rattles my bones, shakes my knees.
I am reminded of a time gone by
   when sleeping in a boat we lie.
Wild waves crashing against the prow
   torturing my brain, contorting my brow–
Would we make it safely to shore?
   I read the signs, I'm not so sure.
I look at him and say no word -
   to stop the storm. Is that absurd?
Our eyes meet and in a split second
   my whole life, in my head I amend.
Will we live, or will we die
   beneath the ocean floor lie?

He looks at me back, his eyes serene -
   What does that calm, reassuring gaze mean?

Does it mean we shall be spared,
in this tempest, its temper flared?
Is it possible that he dost know
what his words do not show?
His tall, strong countenance serene
in this storm, weather extreme.
Boat rocking from side to side,
how can he so still abide?
We'll all be lost, we shan't be found -
hit by waves of fear, doubt profound.
The mental anguish and the pain -
hit the boat, like nails of rain.
Will we capsize?
Or will he realize?

He is the lord of all the storms -
   His power beyond all nature's norms.
   He calms the storm - one command,
   stops the wind's resonance and sound
   thundering through the crashing waves
   the storm subsides - our lives he saves.
   An order uttered in faith - its power
   the forces of nature does empower.

Calm ensued
   Spirits renewed
   boat re-calibrated
   storm liberated
   Clouds shifting
   Waters sifting
   back into the sea

All is calm -
as calm as can be.

Safely we reach the shore -
Fear and doubt are no more.
He chides us for our lack of faith
and laughs, as we are now safe.
For the same as he calms down the storm
we also could do that, since we were born.
But, our power we have sadly lost-
amidst brainwashing at great cost.
As when storms hit us in the now and here
the resonance of our voice loud and clear
has the power storms to dissipate -
His example, we must imitate.
We like him too, storms can subside
if only we remembered, if only we tried.
If our sacred innate divine power we recall,
then storms in our lives, shall be storms no more.

Chapter 24

The Sound Summons

My Spirit overflows with your sweet presence
   my body reverberates within your divine Essence.
   I sit on the earth - in a quiet place, still space -
   the most sacred sound Nada, me does embrace.

If only all were aware of your presence
   feeling your pure, divine Essence,
   reverberating in the depths of their Being,
   feeling, hearing what their eyes aren't seeing!

Perhaps, if you whispered softly through
   a gentle sensuous caressing breeze, to
   sing in their ears a sweet melody,
   each of their own bespoke beauty?

What if you shouted out aloud,
   with bolts of lightning through a thunder cloud
   and told them in no uncertain terms,

they really belonged to the heavenly realms?

What if your song through sound waves resounds
   bringing to their awareness pure heavenly sounds,
   notes unsurpassed, unheard of ever before,
   sweet symphonies singing of heaven's lore?

Would they listen, would they tune in
   to the sacred music playing within?
   It sings to each of their own unique divine nature,
   reminding them they are not their physical stature,
   as it wilts and decays this transitional bodily form,
   that unfortunately is at the moment, the norm.

So, instead of building temples of stone,
   why don't you come to God alone
   in the living temple of your heart -
   God's sacred creation, His work of art,
   singing His glory with songs of praise?
   Listen to that sacred celestial sound -
   and see what it softly says.

III

Part Three

Mother and Son

Mary go, go, go!
We go with you so
Do not worry or be scared
All your prayers shall be heard

And know that the love with which He loves Mother and Son,
Is the love with which He loves everyone -
Wherever you are, whatever you do,
know and feel in your heart that God loves you too.

Let these few verses inspire you to see
His infinite love for you and for me.
Whoever you are, wherever you may be
experience for yourself and examine carefully,
See if it resonates within silently

Chapter 25

<u>The Prodigal Daughter</u>

"Son, what would you have me do?
My heart beats soundly with love for you.
As when I stood under that damn'd cross -
Your Father's handmaid – He is the boss!

I lovingly offer up my life and my light,
in my being may He find sheer delight.
Praying that every mantra muttered,
every prayer of praise uttered,
every single meditation and song
may to my sacred Creator belong.

Approaching the heavenly portal once more
slowly, yet surely opening the door,
allowing God's Law and divine will
to fill my whole being, until -
once again I know His presence,
deep within me – my Essence.

I very almost lost my chance –
   yet a gentle nudge and a diddy dance,
   from the heavens in my heart
   showed me where to start -
   following the thread
   the signs I read
   of what I must do
   where I must go
   who I must see -
   realized to be.

By sacred God's pure grace and love unending,
   my story's not ended in despair never-ending,
   for He has turned my return and home-coming
   into a lush feast of a prodigal daughter becoming.
   And like the prodigal son when he came back,
   we hugged, kissed and He cut me some slack!
   Life, love, peace, bliss and harmony,
   now me always joyfully accompany
   everywhere I go, whatever I do
   they are there, and so is He too.
   I realise the past is gone – done and dusted -
   God's own love and grace my sin have busted.
   I am jubilantly happy and finally at peace,
   my karmic debt and wretchedness released.

I can't believe my luck
   as out of the pit, unstuck -
   I am free to roam the Earth with glee

that was created for you and for me.
To walk once again with my Son
reunited now - we are one.
Not to be apart ever again,
his peace and joy in me remain.
Through tears and laughter,
sadness and mirth -
a resurrection, my brand new birth,
overcoming murder by the knife,
coming back again fully alive to life."

And as mother and Son are reunited
the mother's love is reignited.
The Son's jumping over the moon
coming back in his power soon
to his mother, and to all his lambs and sheep
who in his Father's sheepfold safe he'll keep
and secure. Safe from harms way,
never to be brutally prized away.
All come together united in the law,
the law of Love - as he foresaw.

And His own beloveds, together they dine -
on heavenly manna. Their beings shine
brighter than stars and suns,
resting where fresh water runs.
They shine and shimmer
with His grace glimmer
in the sacred garden of mystery,
an epic end to a very long story.
A happy ending all around -

a victorious joyful ringing sound
welcomes throngs to a sacred space,
coming from every country and race -
the gates wide open,
the windows too,
follow the music
as it guides you.

The melody plays
  the peace stays,
  the perfume smells
  of Love it tells!
  The laughter sings,
  its rapture rings -
  The rejoicing springs
  its angelic wings.
  The mansion is filling
  with those willing
  to come back to sacred Life-Love-Light,
  to the sacred Father-Mother-Son's delight.

The music's playing
  hips are swaying
  Dancing forever
  from God never
  to be separated
  a union cemented .
  Now and always living as one
  as the course of time will run
  an eternity of bliss -
  Earth and Heaven kiss

whilst beings are adoring
their Creator's praise soaring,
high into divine sacred ears,
singing away everyone's fears.

A final reunion.
   An end to delusion
   An end to anguish
   An end to anger
   An end to fear
   An end to violence
   An end to jealousy
   An end to envy
   An end to poverty
   An end to hate
   An end to greed
   An end to lust
   An end to injustice
   An end to prejudice
   An end to war.

A new dawn dawns, verily,
   peace, love, joy, dance in unity.
   Safe and free from fear,
   Living in Creator – His voice hear -
   His Love feel enfolding your heart,
   You've made it home. Never depart
   from Him or from His sacred Law,
   be present now and forevermore.

And as The Father-Mother love The Son-

They've always loved and will love everyone.
Come now, without much further ado -
do your laces up or buckle your shoe.
Hurry!
Time's of the essence, let's all get moving
ecstatically dancing, let's all get grooving.
Filled with sacred Life-Love-Light
rest, sleep and have a *good night* -
sweet dreams and sleep tight.
Finally, rest in the fact we are all one -
sacred Father-Mother, us and the Son.

Chapter 26

<u>Glastonbury Tor</u>

I climbed up the steep hill
   albeit, at one point got stuck
   at about half-way up.
   Do I continue to climb
or is it time
to give up,
   head to a pub?
I bite the bullet and
continue clambering up
despite the path being
slippery with mud.
And to my utter and sheer surprise
arrive the back way to the rise,
of the Tor from the side -
where the path is narrow, not wide.
I felt within the soles of my feet,
as I stood where the Mary and the Michael lines meet -
a strange sensation, a pacifying peace

a new life arising, on life a new lease!
A joy arising
as peace abiding
a freedom true
in me grew
and in the soles of my feet,
where the Mary and the Michael lines meet.

I looked around
   a melodious sound
   rang in my ears
   sang away my fears.
   A red rose petal I found -
   as velvety and as smooth as the sound
   that reverberated through the soles of my feet
   where the Mary and the Michael lines meet.

I, Mary climbed up and as I landed
   a heavenly presence upon me descended.
   The Lord Mikaal, or Michael to you,
   came to welcome and to greet me, too.
   "I've been waiting Mariya,
   I've been waiting for you.
   You were brought to the Tor
   to meet me, for
   here your beautiful beloved Son walked,
   whilst the hills listened still as he talked.
   Birds sang their simple song -
   it was perfect - nothing wrong."
   I felt the warm welcome in the soles of my feet,

where the Mary and the Michael lines meet.

"I, Lord Mikaal or Michael as you will,
   walked with you always, walk with you still.
   My aim you and your Son to be reunited
   your love for him to be reignited
   on his favourite spot of all time -
   He shall make your whole being shine,"
   and a luminous light shone around the soles
   of my feet,
   where the Mary and the Michael lines meet.

My Being rejoices at the presence of my Son,
   the Son of God, the most sacred One.
   And most grateful and thankful am I
   that you Mikaal, have not passed me by.
   But, brought me back to my beloved Son
   so that now we can all be one.
   "On the hill he too had walked,"
   the Hill declared to the soles of my feet,
   there, just where the Mary and the Michael lines meet.

"I must now depart, Mariya my dearest soul,
   as I have gladly achieved my desired goal.
   Mother and Son are finally reunited -
   their love for each other now reignited.
   The bond is tried and tested, too -
   You love him and he loves you,"
   whispered Lord Mikaal softly to the soles of my feet,
   the message reverberated through my being to greet
   the land, where the Mary and the Michael lines meet.

Chapter 27

The First Night

You held your baby, you held him tight,
  kissed and cuddled him right through the night
  your heartbeat overflowing with love - his birth
  through you - incarnating onto this earth.

He rested his tiny head on your warm-loving chest,
  and suckled silently on your tiny breast.
  Peace enveloped you and him, all around
  choirs of angels singing - the only sound.

A stillness, a tranquility, a peace of heaven
  in the stable -
  whilst Mary, Joseph, shepherds
  and animals were able
  to acknowledge that the Son of God is here born -
  A new way of being he brings, a brand new dawn.

The cow, the ass and the sheep

CHAPTER 27

Him proudly meet and greet!
Lowly stable animals, in a humble abode,
just as the angels said and the prophecy foretold.
The star shone bright
on the baby that night
on God's heart's delight,
shone the golden light
illuminating his face,
with a divine grace.

A warmth ensues
   the cold subdues
   the baby rests
   in linen vests
   wrapped up tight
   through that first night.

Chapter 28

The Mother in Bethlehem

I held him tight, close to my chest,
   as he drank milk from my tiny breast
   my heart with a joy and love over-flowing
   as the stable with the star's lights a-glowing.
   A deep peace envelopes the cave -
   where God to humanity, His first-born gave.

Stillness, as the shepherds adored,
   glory as peace 'd been restored.
   Heaven has come down to Earth to,
   show the way of truth to me and to you.
   The shepherds and their faithful sheep
   warm peace in the stillness did keep.

And as he nestled to my breast,
   Him and I and all the rest -
   felt heaven's portal open wide
   a Presence with the Son reside.

CHAPTER 28

He suckled slowly, his first earthly meal,
making his incarnation much more real.

I looked at him, in wonder and awe,
my heart rejoicing, at what my eyes saw,
My heart warm, as he fed on milk raw.
My hands held him tight,
for he is the Light
for us all to follow,
today and tomorrow.
The Son of God, this little babe
who of Life and Love is made,
will one day show us all the way,
and to all one day he shall say:

"Mark my words, I speak sacred truth -
I know what I'm saying, although a mere youth.
The sacred Father-Mother love you dearly,
their hearts over-flowing to the brim, clearly
want all to come back home to the heavenly estate -
I tell you all this, on their mandate
so that where I am, there you are too,
you can all come, be there, yes you!
Bring all of your heart, mind, soul, body,
tall, short, fat, slim, dark, fair, everybody.
Come back to the heart of God sacred, supreme
with a golden grace let your whole being beam.
I will show you all how -
We'll all find a way, somehow!
I'll make it easy, as you just follow me
then the way - you'll clearly see.

The blindness from your eyes disappears
wisdom, clarity, intuition, insight reappears.
You will be renewed and born once more,
to enjoy the grace of God and Him adore."

And, I, Mary, his mother on Earth did ponder,
   these events in awe and wonder
   as heaven's Son in my arms lay,
   keeping him safe come what may.
   My heart aglow with a love divine,
   for my God and for this son of mine.

So grateful for Joseph's presence too, as he
   is forgotten, often, in the whole story.
   His firm, faithful presence did us strengthen
   throughout his life, I do need to mention.
   He stayed honest, fair, present and true,
   loving the Son of God and in him imbue
   a love for the skill of working with wood,
   beautiful carvings, his hand could
   wield. He taught the Son this trade,
   so He too, intricate carvings made.

In the stable Joseph stayed,
   and on him my head I laid.
   As he beheld the Son and his mum,
   it's like he beheld everyone,
   whom would welcome the Son,
   who to Earth had just come.

Humble, yet firm,

gentle and sweet-
here's where Heaven and Earth meet.
In this stable - in a cave -
The sacred Son his life gave.
For on his birthday celebrated,
is the Earth's balance re-calibrated.

The portals to the heavens opened wide,
  so that humanity may no longer hide
  in hatred, anger, anguish, fear-
  Resting only in Life and Love, as Light is here.

Chapter 29

<u>Mother Son and Everyone</u>

Mother and Son reunited
   their love for each other reignited.
   Always there, but by sin obscured -
   now it shines bright – fully renewed.
   His heart is full and over-flowing
   Her heart rejoices in the knowing
   that he is here -
   her son, her dear.

To him she joyously clings -
   her soul, his praises sings.
   She is overjoyed at the prospect
   that now her soul he will protect
   from untruths, false dogmas, doctrines,
   relentlessly ringing their deafening sirens.
   The Truth shall set her free -
   not just her, but everybody.

CHAPTER 29

Her whole being remembers clearly
  when as a child he wandered freely
  into thick woods climbing up trees
  wading through rivers up to his knees
  cheekily grinning, so full of life -
  free from worry, free from strife.
  She would hold him close to her,
  as Mother Earth, their sustainer
  would teach him a thing or two -
  something old, something new.

He, a great son
  second to none.
  Loving all dearly
  unto death clearly.
  His Love
  above
  beyond
  all din -
  His grace
  above
  beyond
  all sin.
  Rupture will be arriving very soon -
  with a whishing bang, a whopping boom!

The world awaits patiently with joyous
  anticipation -
  humanity's ascension - sanctification -
  all realized in their divine state,
  each gifted a brand new slate;

all renew what has been smashed;
restoring hopes which had been crushed,
filling the whole Earth below and above
with a sublime, divine unconditional Love.

Chapter 30

<u>The Two Mothers</u>

Mary, humble mother of the Son whilst on Earth,
   sharing motherhood with the divine Earth
   for his birth -
   Both their hearts bounteously overflowing
   with the love of their sacred child knowing
   they have mothered the Son of God divine,
   by God's own sacred plan and grand design.
   Both present, as the divine plan does unfold,
   a lot of these stories are left hidden - untold!

The rapturous joy at his birth they both felt
   and in deep adoration, both of them knelt-
   Enveloped in peace, Mary and Aurora Divine
   are heard in unison singing: "He is not mine,
   but belongs to God divine, up above and below,
   incarnated on earth, His Father's love to sow.
   And although through Mary he came and he stayed,
   both Mary and Aurora he graciously obeyed.

Aurora's angels surrounded both him and her (Mary),
and for humanity Aurora's throngs of angels do care.

Aurora divine watched with joy and sheer ecstasy
Mary's love for their Son, she pondered joyously.
A love deeply touching sweet-smelling of roses,
a love although strong, as delicate as posies.
Aurora relished the fun which was had,
on sweet summer nights when their hearts
were so glad.
Mother Mary sweet stories, her Yeshua she told
and he listened transfixed, as of heroes so bold -
who fought without fear, to bring justice and peace,
the baddies get rid of, the goodies release!
Stories of those who in devotion to their loving Creator,
embraced and proclaimed Him, in love, as their Maker.
And the Son intently listened to his sweet mother's
tales,
such lessons of God's Love for males and females,
for the tall, the short, the fat, the dark or fair -
for the strong, the weak and those in disrepair.

Aurora watched silently Mary teaching him to pray,
as she tucked him up in bed at the end of the day -
to trust in His Father-Mother divine come what may,
be grateful for life's blessings, the *Our Father* to say.
He loved her prayers, the sweet Son of God
listened intently,
silently relishing -
her company cherishing
her motherhood adoring

as prayers came pouring
forth.

They joked, laughed, played and had fun,
   love shone brightly from mother to son.
   The son himself, his mother adored -
   in Mary's heart such stories 're still stored.
   In silence Aurora watched the two together
   both their hearts as light as a feather -
   running, jumping and skipping around,
   their laughter the most joyous sound
   to Queen Aurora's silent ears-
   these two dearly beloved dears
   brought joy and made life sweet.
   At dawn her angels both did meet
   with blessings true the day greet -
   with a sweet morning's dew
   and other blessings too.
   The angels by day joined in the fun,
   as he toddled around, the day 'd begun.
   They sang their hearts out, him and Mary sweet,
   the day with delicious music each did greet!

Chapter 31

<u>The Son to his Mother I</u>

Mother, mother let me whisper in your ear,
    dearest mother, know that I am here.
    I love you hanini* with a love so sublime
    and care for you with a compassion divine.
    No mother is greater, than this mother of mine.

You sang to me sweetly, when I just a babe
    gurgling sweet noises of joy I had made.
    We played together and what fun we had
    albeit, sometimes it was hard and quite sad
    especially when Joseph died, alone we were left,
    I remember you mum, feeling sad and bereft.

Your sweet-smelling smile an exquisite perfume
    I'd always smell your aura as you entered a room.
    Your sweetness abides, not just for me -
    You were generous, sweet and all could see
    you were the best mother, you could ever be.

CHAPTER 31

You tended me gently, with compassionate care
   nobody would hurt me, nobody would dare,
   as you'd come forth charging like an angry bull
   with a bucket or two of cold water full,
   your protective loving kindness so beautiful.

Chapter 32

The Son to His Mother II

Mother, release all anger, anguish, agony, pain,
   My Calvary shall never be in vain!
   The hammer's down, the nails are in
   to free each and every one from sin.
   I lay there, all bl**dy meek and lame,
   Taking on humanity's shame.

The Father-Mother and the Holy Spirit look on.
   They do love me, they love the Son.
   Yet, that soul-contract I had signed
   the whole of Calvary pre-designed –
   How that treacherous murder to avoid?
   I was getting ever-increasingly paranoid.

Nevertheless, die I did, this is for sure -
   the beast's hell mauled me to the floor.
   On a cross they splayed my body beaten,
   which by worms, I knew shan't be eaten.

As now I am alive - I live once more,
I wipe away what was before!
A new shoot springs, a fresh new start
God's very own brand-new work of art.
A new Being for you and them to enjoy -
freedom, justice, peace, love and joy.

To you dearest mother, I say these words –
    we protect and provide as for these flocks of birds.
    To you dearest mother, who has loved me so,
    I apologise, for I did have to suddenly go –
    not in a way which a mother would dream,
    left you wondering what did all of this mean.
    I am so sorry my dearest mother true,
    that when I died on the cross, so did you.

In silence you did suffer your pain,
    so that your life was never the same.
    I am so sorry that your heart simple, pure,
    pain beyond breaking point had to endure.
    An agony that would rip your tender heart apart -
    A jagged dagger right through your mother's heart!
    It left you searching, finding a way –
    To let the pain go, sometimes going astray.
    Trying to find some meaning in it all,
    your suffering did your progress stall.
    You tried to bring lost souls to me,
    so that the fruits of our agony -
    would not devoid of meaning be.

Now Love enlarges your heart, expands your soul-
   to heal yourself, your life-time goal.
   My Father's love, all your anguish transforms
   into joy - as He does all of life's storms.
   Your heart, it yearns to be set free,
   yearns for a peace and tranquility
   filled with love for all humanity,
   your wishes shall come true.
   My dearest mum, I love you!
   Your Son
   Yeshua

Chapter 33

<u>The Son to his Mother III</u>

"You gave me life and nursed me with loving care,
  your love flooded my being - freshened the air.
  But now your Yeshua is a fully grown man,
  about to fulfill his soul-purpose's plan."

Yeshua's been trying to get you back to him
  to be free from fear, anguish and sin.
  His heart's longing's to be reunited,
  your love for him to be reignited,
  as like in the days of old,
  as the story's been told;
  united together once again - as one -
  the desolate mother to her dear Son.

"I've waited for many years
  shed torrents of tears -
  as you mum did not heed my call,
  it were as if you didn't care at all!
  From the truth inside you, you hid,

till to come back to me, you decided.

Slowly over the years back to me you returned,
 many paths to choose from; options to be
 discerned.
 Soon after you quickly clambered through the
 gate -
 almost - almost - almost - a bit too late!
 Just about got onto the last boat which sailed,
 just as well it was deliberately delayed.
 The boat you did not miss, but on it got
 just in the nick of time, missed it not!
 And once aboard, you prayed and prayed
 petitions of love to your Creator relayed.
 Your home-coming joyously celebrated,
 a home-coming so long-awaited.
 Joy beyond words filled my heart,
 coupled with a promise we'd never part.
 I'd hoped and waited you would return
 leaving the desolate roads you did sojourn.

I know you love me, mumsie dear
 this to me is crystal clear.
 Your life you have now turned around
 helped by Nada, that sacred sound.
 This melodious music of the universe
 grew and grew,
 leading you back home to the Love
 you once knew.
 And once back home within you came,
 then nothing, nothing - stayed the same!

Your Christ-hood embraced, you transformed,
your heart, mind, body, soul newly formed.
We rejoice in your new birth-
we celebrate here, full of mirth.
A new Mary - a new mum to me,
a new Mother Mary for all to see.

Dancing and singing I rejoice
at your wise and timely choice.
But now mumsie dear, it's getting late,
and it'll soon be time to open the gate -
to the dream world. Rest your wearied head,
on a soft bed, no tears of guilt or regret shed.
In your dreams, I shall come -
I'll come to you mum
so that you can recall
the teachings of old and more.
You'll know what to do,
where to go,
what to say -
My Spirit goes in front, before and ahead,
for 'I am the way,' is what I once said.

So, saunter ahead tall and straight
and this time, pleeeease don't be late!
Get on the boat, sail with me
across rivers, walk on the sea."

Chapter 34

<u>The Heavenly Father to Mother Mary</u>

Dearest Mother Mary,
  I'm so so sorry -
  please know this,
  please, please do!
  I didn't know it'll kill you all-
  that treacherous murder - a tall
  order, Mary, you were given -
  now all your sins are forgiven.
  It's taken far too long to heal -
  A restoration, a brand new seal
  is suddenly stamping My creation,
  embossed on the heart of every nation
  is ME -sacred Life- Love- Light divine,
  all shall know that they are mine.

At this moment my Son is fully arisen
  from the ensnaring matrix's prison.
  He is healed and fully restored,

in humble hearts simply adored.
He is the Consciousness of Light
your own within, He shall ignite.
His living light-presence in those who love him -
Frees from fear itself and from fear of death.
His living light-presence in those who don't,
wants to shine forth, but if blocked it won't!

The murder from long ago now forgotten.
   A new reality is now begotten.
   Some work still needs to be done
   so many more to Love must come.

Although he doesn't suffer any more,
   he would like more to come through
   the portal door.
   To come and enjoy the sumptuous
   heavenly feast -
   from the very high to the very least-
   all are invited.
   Some decline,
   some are busy,
   some come to dine.

Chapter 35

<u>Mother and Son - A Dialogue</u>

"You are finally here mumsie, dear,
   speak to me, let me lend you my ear.
   Rest your wearied head on my chest,
   that's it, great! And get some rest
   from the wretchedness which demons lay
   in your path,
   leaving a dark delirious aftermath.
   Rest your old weary soul, my mum,
   I'll let you know – this is your Son.
   Abandon the wretchedness, do come
   rest in my heart, as we are now one."

"I can feel your gentle heartbeat,
   as my head and your heart meet.
   I can hear the Nada sound -
   throughout my mind, body, soul resound.
   I'm glad to rest in your peace so tranquil,
   protected from all powers of evil."

CHAPTER 35

"And as in the days of old-
   you protect me from the cold.
   When, I, a tiny babe in your loving arms,
   you held me tight out of harm's way
   steering dense energy and evil away.
   And as I had rested my tiny ear,
   on your chest, I, too could hear
   the gentle rhythm of your love playing
   a melody of a joyful peace saying
   that you, Mother - mother of mine -
   loved me then and now with a love sublime.
   The past wretchedness gone and buried,
   beautiful memories of our love untarried.
   When two thousand years ago,
   your love in earthly ways did show,
   here now two thousand years after,
   your love surpasses death, alive ever-after.
   It survived all the the traps that'd been laid-
   to trip you up, your path to me way-layed,
   stopping you from coming back
   taking you off the rightful track -
   trapping you in a dark, black sack
   and because of the darkness and despair
   in there,
   you wouldn't be able to go anywhere.
   They set snares, but couldn't see
   the formidable love you have for me
   and I for you, mother dear -
   I am here... have no fear, have no fear.
   Let's not worry 'bout what went on before
   stay in sacred Life-Love-Light forevermore.

Its nature sacred, it is divine,
this love for you, Mother of mine."

"U Superjur and mum and Nanna Nina -
Ikollkom hniena minna, itolbu ghalina.
Kunu mieghi f'dal-granet li gejjin,
tghidulix li intom ghajjenin!
Ejjew bi hgarkom, ghinuni f'li gej
bi grazzji, kuragg u l-paci tal-Feddej.
Mank nista' narakom, naqra zghira,
immiskom
inxommkom
inhosskom, dazgur.
Kif intom ma Ibni ta' Alla l-Mahtur,
thossuH, tarawH u tkellmuH.
Kemm hi safja dik ir-ruh,
illi Lilu thoss fil-fond tal-qalb,
u Lilu tkellem dejjem fit-talb.
Inhobbu lil Ibni, ta' Alla l-Mahtur,
Imzejjen bil-Glorja ta' Salvatur.
Inhobbu lil Ibni b'imhabba tal-genn,
U l-imhabba Tieghu ghalija dejjem hi kenn.
Mhux li kien inhossu f'dirghajja
bhal fl-ewwel Milied, meta gew ir-rghajja,
u rawH fuq sidri jistrieh,
jiekol u jixrob qatiegh -
halli guh u ghatx ma jbatix.
L-imhabba tieghi bhal gharix
ittieh kemm mill-bard ta' barra,
kenn mill-qalb li minn Alla tizgarra
kenn mill-hruxija tal-qlub maghluqin -

offrulu mhabba safja, bhal ikel bnin."

This poetry flows forth in Maltese. It still expresses her love for her Son and how she hopes that it offers Him solace and warmth, protecting him not just from the cold in the cave in Bethlehem, but from cold hearts that do not want to know him and his Love. The Mother urges everybody to offer their love as a pure offering like that of a wholesome meal.

Chapter 36

<u>Mother to Son</u>

I am grateful beyond words can say,
   or any message can ever relay.
   For I am back home where I belong,
   so sorry Son it's taken so long.
   But, the plan is now being fulfilled
   as my home-coming with joy is filled
   may it benefit everyone -
   Humanity, me and God's sacred plans, Son.

I'm so delighted to wake up and see
   that really, you've never left me.
   Through the trauma of it all, I lost the path,
   the unfortunate outcome of its aftermath,
   I wasn't able to stay the same -
   down many a deserted road and lonely lane -
   lost - no direction - overwhelmed with shame.

Your love within me shall always remain,

although I'd changed; I'm not the same.
All the anguish I can feel melting,
grace like rain comes down pelting
filling my emptied soul with Love
so that it is below as is above.

My Son, your sacred divine light
  radiates through my being bright
My soul is alchemised, reformed -
all trauma into love transformed.
Your presence in me fulfilled
the raging storm within stilled.
As gusts of cold wind fear flows,
Not now - not toward me blows,
and when it does, I do not fear,
for Life-Love-Light divine is here.

My Son arisen, my Son alive
  soon humanity shall arrive
at the point when it turns to You,
that time I hope is almost due
justice and peace 'll be revived -
the Christ-Consciousness within realized.

A Son whose love for all is beyond measure -
  whose presence in one's heart - a treasure
trove of bliss and joy – beyond any price -
Our Lord Yeshua, Jesias , Jesus The Christ.

IV

Part Four

<u>Back Home – Where We Belong</u>

Back home where we belong,
hymns of praise - our song-
peace, bliss and joy abound
at Love's calling - a joyous sound.
In our heart's and mind's eye we can see
and know, sacred Life-Love-Life within you and me.
A heaven born on a renewed Earth
is now being given birth.

Chapter 37

<u>The One in All - The All in One</u>

Rose incense wending its way to me,
   so that where you are, so shall I be.
   Specks of dust dancing in the light,
   frivolous fairies twirling in delight.

They come to greet me
   and whisper softly:
   "Mary, we welcome you home
   to your divine heavenly throne.
   Not of the human earthly plane
   neither in the heights of heaven,
   as we'll explain!

Within the inner world - deep in the heart,
   is a presence…um…where shall we start?
   The Essence from which all emerges -
   as Life-Love-Light to one point converges
   within this expansive, boundary-free space

abides the whole of the human race.
And not just that, but all universes too-
All there is without - is also within you.

A whole universe is the human heart.
   In it all is one - all a part
   of the sacred bigger whole -
   a shard of this - our soul -
   unseen through human sight,
   is sacred Christ-Conscious Light
   through the third eye on our forehead,
   is seen what the naked eye doesn't get.
   Like a wave is a part of the ocean always,
   whether it rages, crashes or gently plays.

Resting in The Sacred One…
   the heart pulsates in its presence
   knows it, as its inherent Essence -
   basks in its bliss,
   Peace and Joy kiss.

The Spirit within the heart and mind,
   when this Essence they finally find
   leap up for joy - portals open wide -
   putting fear, anger, shame and guilt aside.
   Swirling body, heart, soul, Spirit and mind,
   a dance of unity to the song of One chimed.

The breath joins in
   expanding within
   our inner Universe

CHAPTER 37

enthrallingly diverse
pure blissful deep
where angels keep
their gifts sweet.
Fear subsides
Spirit abides
in the depths of each soul,
a unique part of the Whole.

The One heart and mind permeates,
   whilst the body an illusion creates,
   one of scattered pieces and division,
   our perception needs revision.
   That which is perceived out there
   separates uniquely in him or in her
   expressed through many is The One,
   present in each and everyone.
   A presence transcending body -
   the essence of everything, everybody
   permeating everything - everywhere.
   Not just in here, or just out there,
   but equally present in a mustard seed,
   a blossomed flower or a wilting weed.

All illusions drop,
   deceptions stop.
   We experience being ONE -
   Spirit, heart, mind, body, breath,
   Father-Mother-Sacred Spirit
   and The Son.

Chapter 38

A New Heaven - A New Earth

Soon he comes to gather his nation,
   his beloved souls, without hesitation.
   From east, west, north, south they assemble
as part of the sacred Son's ensemble.
In Light are the seeds he generously sows,
as abundant Love and Life on Earth flows.
The weeds which desecrate the garden floor
are alchemised and are weeds no more,
as healing medicine their true nature must
be realized; and we humans this must trust,
knowing that for every illness, Aurora divine
has a natural, healing free remedy sublime.
Away from synthetic poison we must go,
earth's garden persists to organically grow
with grass lush green as never before seen
dazzling green blades' bright silvery sheen.
Roses, dandelions, buttercups, elderflower,
all have the potency and the power

CHAPTER 38

to make our bodies' ailments right,
radiating with a life, love, light bright.
Trees in blossom, pink, white, blue
and many a different colourful hue.

The Son stands at the door of his lovingly
   tended garden,
   of which he is now the most
   gracious warden.
A garden delightful - a garden perfect,
in it compassion, peace, bliss, joy, respect.
He welcomes all as they leap through the door,
fear, anguish, anger, pain are no more.
Roses adorn the floor and the portal door,
exquisite scents not ever smelt before.
In they enter – they joyfully come,
from everywhere, each and everyone.
He welcomes them anew,
whether many or just a few,
who make it through the open garden door -
Their loving Creator they devotedly adore.
They dance for joy, with ecstasy leap
as Oneness with their God they keep.
The water shimmers silver and gold,
the Water of Life, they have been told
for them to bathe in day and night,
making their beings shine ever so bright.
The birds all singing a welcoming song -
joining in the melody of the angelic throng.
A radiant blue bird with golden wings,
songs of praise to God it sings -

a thanks-giving gift to its Creator
an act of perfect adoration of its Maker.
A silken pink rose joins in the hymns of praise
all the newcomers to welcome and embrace.
All are in communion divine and perfect peace
the newcomers, the birds, the herons, the geese.
All living as one in harmony
all living as one happy family
all living in God and in this heavenly Kingdom,
partaking of sacred Life-Love-Light and wisdom.
The past is past – gone and forgotten
a heaven on a new Earth is begotten.
These faithful souls, these pure of heart,
forever and always of sacred God a part.

Chapter 39

Hallelujah

Yeshua has won – well done Son!
   We know it is done.
   Your passion hasn't been in vain
   as God's grace, a refreshing rain
   falls on Earth, on those returning to grace
   quite a huge chunk of the human race.
   Enough to make it all worthwhile,
   making the hosts of heaven smile …
   Enough to deck the halls of heaven with guests
   their beings shine, as their weary heart rests …

A day of great grace all around,
   bugles playing a victorious sound.
   A heaven established here on Earth,
   creation's been given a brand new birth.
   Oh, it is so dazzling to hear and see -
   hearts overflowing in ecstasy!
   It's happening now as we live the prophecy,

of all that soon shall come to be.
Light's grace is descending -
Creation finally ascending.
Some Earthlings, fallen panicking.
Beings of Light within them knowing
that the time is here and it is now -
that their good shepherd is here, somehow.
He comes to gather all his sheep
flooding them with waves of love deep.
Now in the safety of his unbounded pen,
they know Love divine just like when
he had held them once so close
their life-force shone and rose,
as did their inner equanimity.
He always had had the ability
to make them like him, shine -
showing them how to resurrect,
like him - their souls divine!
In this heaven on this new Earth of his,
there's no pain or suffering, only bliss.

It's what we've all been yearning for -
   Our pure state of being - before the fall.
   Back to our state of pure perfection,
     our brand new start – our resurrection.

Hallelujah! Rejoice!
   In this new state of being repose
   in its pure harmony
   its sweet tranquility
   a state blissfully divine -

CHAPTER 39

by God's loving grand design.

Chapter 40

Oh Blessed Day!

Thank you for many a warning sign
   as the energies of Life-Love-Light realign;
   ample time before the gates shut,
   and the Book of Life in half is cut -
   souls ascending into dimensions new,
   not many lost, hopefully only a few.
   It all makes Yeshua's death worthwhile,
   puts on his angelic face a smile
   as he now leads his faithful nation,
   generation after generation.

In they come, fervently worshiping at his feet
   this is where God and human divinity meet.
   They just want to be in him,
   pure inside - and free from sin.
   In this new sacred universe pure,
   they all rest, all peacefully secure.
   They come in earnest, him adore,

he loves them all down to the core.

Oh, blessed day you are come -
  to welcome the heavenly Son's
  new kingdom of Love on Earth -
  peace, equanimity, joy and mirth,
  envelop them all – these beings -
  a life beyond their wildest dreams.

Oh, blessed day you are come -
  a new dawn dawns, a new day's begun.
  The radiance of the sun so bright
  emitting a Life, Love-giving Light,
  sending each and every ray,
  deep into our Being to stay.

Oh, blessed day you are come -
  long-awaited by everyone!
  Hills, mountains, rivers and falls,
  our sacred land that to us all calls,
  in excited anticipation -
  to a broken Earth, reparation
  a healing, a repair, a restoration
  yearned for, in eager expectation.

Oh, blessed day you are come-
  To welcome the heavenly Son!
  A new dawn dawns – a new day's begun,
  long-awaited by everyone!

Chapter 41

A Celebration

Skipping, dancing, leaping in the air
   heaven on earth is already here
   in the depths of your heart it is -
   filling you with a celestial bliss.
   Let's celebrate and have some fun,
   you, me, my Son and everyone.
   Let's jump for joy, way up high -
   up to the heavens, let our spirits fly.
   Twirling, singing, shrieks of laughter,
   joy, love, peace, bliss forever after.
   Just like a fairy-tale finally come true -
   your divine nature, you realized - you!

Through the portal door they bound
   back home, the way they've found.
   And whether weary
   or blithely bouncy,
   whether dreary

or somewhat flouncy -
different bodies, in different sizes,
have now come to claim their prizes.
Their feet have touched the ground
some with a thump or a silent sound,
their spirits soar up high -
in joyful celebration cry.

Jumping for exultation,
 with no boundary or limitation
 these souls excitedly bound in
 through the portal door wherein
 a new peace graces the heart's terrain
 back home to Life-Love-Love once again.

Chapter 42

<u>God Speaks through the Mist in Avalon</u>

God speaks to me in the mist today
   an important message to relay
   shrouded in magic and mystery
   a message seeped in this place's history.

Up on the side of the Tor,
   further up upon the moor
   veiled in a stilled silence
   a message is revealed -
   from the chaos concealed,
   delivered to a lowly maid
   as she prays in the shade.
   God suddenly begins to speak,
   to this maiden humble, meek.

"I have come to you today
   to say -
   that come what may
   in the forthcoming days

amidst the misty haze
I shall be with you all.

My will, guides
  My Peace, strengthens
  My Joy, enlivens
  My Presence, enlightens
  My Love protects -
  all of My beloved ones who
  love Me like I love them too.
  Do not be scared -
  just keep standing
  unafraid - in the
  sweet shade
  of my protection
  in its perfection
  power and might,
  day and night
  know my Presence,
  It is your Essence.

For some it will be a
  death dark, slow-
  violent shaking as their bodies blow
  out any light, want it removed -
  their actions not by love approved.
  Their lives dreary, dreadful, dark
  their bodies weak, lacking spark.
  Yet, those beloved ones who to Me come,
  maybe many, maybe some,
  My Heart will welcome into its core -

where refreshing pure waters of Life flow.
Peace and rest they shall once more know.

Show them the way,
    say to them as I say -
    to come to the heart of God now.
    Smell the roses in My Heart
    exquisite perfume, all a part
    and parcel of My Love for You,
    and all of those others who
    rest in Me and I in them.
    Goodbye for now, until then!

Chapter 43

<u>Light Over Darkness Wins</u>

Sacred Light divine our physical being permeates,
   flowing within it in a steady stream it radiates
   like a powerhouse, with this light we forge forth
   congregating from south, east, south and north
   slowly, - but surely gathering speed,
   only of sacred Life-Love-Light the need.
   Each and every soul and sacred spirit,
   welcoming of Life-Love-Light the visit.

Sacred music hums
   to the beat of the drums
   gathering the nations
   without reservations -
   an influx of incoming pilgrims,
   as Light over darkness wins!

Throngs gather by fresh waters flowing -
   dazzling rivers all a-glowing,

shimmering silvery leaves
glowing gleaming sheaves
glittering sight
golden light
silvery bright
smelling sweet
Life-Love-Light meet.
Arms outstretched,
all welcomed back.
Angels shut the portal gate,
for at any rate,
those not here,
are now too late.

Those who are there and then,
   await in anticipation for when
   He calls out their name,
   they are not the same -
   through their bodies,
   their sacredness experienced,
   through their breath,
   their divine nature realized.
   Lived their Life in Light,
   to Love's sheer delight.

Chapter 44

The Mother's Prayer

The ministry of love for which I've been ordained,
  through the Love within me, it's been sustained.
  A delicate pink rose, my being I gift you,
  with it I humbly ask your sacred will do.

I'm welcomed home into your house of joy.
  I'm where I belong. After treacherous toil,
  grief, sadness, anguish, agony and pain -
  Your will be done, may these never again
  assail my being - nearly break my Spirit,
  stretching what seems beyond human limit.

The law of God's Love sacredly inscribed
  into each one's DNA deeply transcribed -
  written in water, flowers, birds, bees,
  in every blade of grass, leaves and trees.
  Sacred Law divine, a sumptuous dish
  to live by it wholly, my utmost wish.

Keep my faith fruitful,
> my love for you beautiful
> my light shining bright for all to see
> bringing them back to You, so let it be.
> Following in your Son's footsteps I come,
> hear this heartfelt prayer from his mum.
> Throngs of angelic beings accompany me here,
> wafting sweet heavenly music into my ear,
> your Spirit spreading all across the Earth,
> giving our Christ-consciousness' new birth.

In full glorious heavenly regalia arrayed,
> His divinity ever-present, living stayed.
> My Son comes in peace to claim his own,
> joined by them now, he is not alone -
> they're full of adoration, ardent devotion,
> their hearts expanding into a loving ocean
> opening up majestically wave after wave -
> each remembering when he his life gave,
> coming to show us how to live on this earth,
> and how to create our own new birth.

May we all bring healing to Aurora's body divine
> bringing her back to wholeness, making her fine
> revive her beauty like the days of yore once more,
> renew her whole being, from her crust to her core.

To bring her body healing, making her whole,
> may this be humanity's sacred new role;
> adoring and protecting her sacred skin and bone,
> humanity has to take responsibility for its home.

CHAPTER 44

Her beauty and sanctity must be adored
   as her mutilated body is healed, restored.
   May she not suffer and die due to greed
   and may everybody acknowledge the need
   for her sustenance, abundantly and freely given,
   may her body now depleted, be forever risen,
   resplendent with dazzling life-force abundant
   A new way of being – the old way's redundant.

Chapter 45

<u>I Am Enough</u>

I am all that I need -
   All's within me like a seed,
   that needs watering and light
   not too dim – not too bright
   to sprout and to flower
   in full blossom -
   Its true power.

The Father-Mother its soil,
   busy angels diligently toil
   to bring it fully to life, so
   to full bloom it shall grow
   its full potential know.

Deep in the dark depths of the Earth below,
   the seed slowly, begins to grow -
   in solitude, silence and stillness.
   New life lightly begins to dance about,
   with rapturous joy it begins to sprout.

CHAPTER 45

All its fragranced beauty celebrate and behold
   her glorious colour and scent renowned-
   an array of diamonds, rubies, sapphires, gold
   the senses tessellate in its beauteous being
   the naked eye's resplendent seeing.

You don't need faith, as you do know
   that as the seeds in the Earth grow,
   and transform into bulbs exquisite -
   you yourself like that gentle flower,
   must go forth and claim your power.

Chapter 46

<u>Forging Forth</u>

Please, sweet, dearly beloved Son
   give strength and courage to your weary mum
   and everything she needs to forge boldly ahead,
   to proclaim the good news, as You'd already said,
   that we are of the beloved sacred God on high,
   our Being is within Him, you do not lie.
   His Essence within, is what is our soul,
   permeates our being, making us whole.

Enlighten our minds
   Open our hearts
   Strengthen our bodies
   Shine through our beings
   Ignite our spark divine.

We have awoken to the tricks of the dark side -
   how they lay secret snares, their hands hide.
   Making them the masters of illusion
   as we all sleep in deceptive delusion

CHAPTER 46

believing their insidious lies no more -
deception comes flying through the door.

Breaking free from their ties
   of their devious deceptive lies
   acknowledging within the truth,
   Freedom and Truth the soul soothe.

Our whole being is now set free
   from lies, deceit, guilt and shame
   we are now able to be -
   on fire with Love's eternal flame.

Chapter 47

<u>The Love of the Father-Mother</u>

The sweetness of the love of the Father-Mother
   for each and every one of us, is like no other.
   They worship the ground we walk on,
   send us their first, only begotten Son.

The heart of the Father-Mother calls -
   to break down barriers, smash down walls
   allowing sacred sweet Love to reign within
   to abide in our hearts and dwell therein.

We must not turn away in haste,
   lest all this Love will go to waste!
   Well, it'll go to someone who relishes it
   and wants to embrace it, every single bit.
   It'll go to the ones who God adore,
   although at times they aren't so sure.
   Yet, they keep the faith and they trust
   this Love and Light within them must

be allowed to shine and shimmer,
filled with hope, its gentle glimmer
their hearts awake.
So much at stake.
Death or life?
Peace or strife?

Awaken now, feel and know
   sweet sacred Love within you glow.
   The Life-Love-Light already within
   shall fill you up, right to the brim!

Chapter 48

The Whisper of your Inner Voice

When as in an apocalypse
   everything suddenly collapses:
   Belief systems, families, finance,
   politics, countries, churches, sects,
   banks - absolutely nothing's left!
   Chaos – with nothing to hold onto,
   to get you through -
   the total disintegration
   of every creed and nation
   a complete decimation -
   of all which has been known,
   heading to a place unknown.
   A moment of great power
   or a moment to despair?
   A moment to disintegrate
   or a moment to repair?
   A moment of sheer brokenness
   and vulnerability,
   or the time to take stock
   and full responsibility?

CHAPTER 48

Looking deep inside -
  nowhere to hide.
  Nothing's left.
  Except -
  your Being
  your Soul,
  your Spirit.

Listening in the stillness of meditation
  to your inner voice's subtle invitation
  in spite the chaos, despite the din
  its quiet, almost inaudible voice within
  reminding us we always have a choice
  in its soft, almost imperceptible voice.
  Amidst the carnage, it guides us,
  softly, simply, without any fuss.

This voice springs out of naught
  when naught is all there remains!
  Most seems absolutely lost -
  Destroyed, devoid of earthly gains,
  with nowhere to go, nowhere to hide,
  only taking refuge in the sound of
  the vibrating silence deep inside.

It feels louder and nearer
  the message gets clearer.
  Truth, strength, courage,
  Life -Love -Light,
  compassion, freedom -
  All dancing a song of joy and gladness

amidst the outer maddening madness
of complete and utter destruction.
Still, softly your inner voice
can be heard whispering:

"You are not weak,
   as you've been told -
   you are not a commodity to be sold,
   you are not a cog in a machine,
   your are not here to just shop and clean,
   you are not stupid or a fool -
   you are not here to be a corporate tool,
   you are not here to serve the government,
   you are not here to be the system's servant!

You are here - listen to me,
   You are here, look and see -
   Open your eyes and ears,
   dust away all fears -
   Allow me to take the lead
   and you shall be free, indeed!
   Allow me to guide your way,
   your inner law of Love obey!
   Allow me to guide you to true authenticity,
   expressing yourself honestly and genuinely.
   Listen to my Voice resounding within you-
   I shall guide you to all that is true.
   Have love and compassion for all others,
   sisters, brothers, fathers, mothers -
   neighbours, friends whoever they may be,
   be kind and compassionate to all and you'll see

that this Love guides you. It sets you free!"

Free from the dark which is now destroyed,
   a new life's created, the old's redeployed.
   The greatest gift of God divine and King -
   deep peace dancing in the depths of our being
   through the new-found union within our hearts
   bringing back into place all the wounded parts
   which have been shattered into a million pieces,
   a deep-rooted peaceful joy our Being seizes.

The heavenly kingdom in our heart's restored,
   our soul within us now reborn, is soared
   through portals bringing its new birth -
   A fully human-divine being treads the earth.
   Go within, where God speaks to the heart. Bow
   to your own Truth within, which you now know.

Chapter 49

With Gratitude

Thank you for journeying with me.
You are now who you are meant to be,
realizing your unique sacred divinity
and its power -
under duress you shall not cower.
With love in my heart I wish you
a path filled with peace and a joy too.
Walk confidently in the days that come,
hard for many, easier for some.
You now have all that you need,
to survive this Armageddon, indeed!

Chapter 50

EPILOGUE

The Red Admiral

It landed on the rocky, dry land
   not on green grass or golden soft sand.
   At first it fluttered its delicate wings,
   as if of life's sadness it silently sings.
   A dainty red admiral in a deserted
   dusty desolate car park.
   A lonely lady - vacant, cheerless -
   her ethereal light-body, wingless.

Delighted at its sight
   she stood still, as it might
   be scared and take flight.
   Time stands still, until …

The Red Admiral momentarily motionless,
   addresses the lonely lady – listless:
   "Fear not, dearest beloved Mary,
   (replace your own name in *Mary's* place)
   for although often quite contrary
   you are loved and full of grace
   but, now let's cut to the chase!
   God has found favour in you -
   He shall make you brand new.
   Do not be scared of any calamity-
   be trusting, still – full of serenity.
   For God promised His protection always
   to those living in sacred Life-Love-Light divine -
   'Nobody shall harm those who are mine!
   Calamity shall strike, tribulation destroy,
   whilst My beloveds, My protection enjoy.

Whilst still a human body inhabiting
   My love throughout it reverberating,
   Strength adorns its every pore,
   Courage roars its mighty roar!
   Your feet shall not be scorched or burnt
   nor your heart, mind, body, soul be hurt.
   For you are cloaked in My Love divine
   within which all is pristine -
   Enveloped in heavenly bliss and peace
   never-ending - they shall never cease.
   Compassionate, kind, unbiased -
   please, My Love readily realize!
   A Love freely given to all,
   I invite you all heed its call.

CHAPTER 50

From the depths of your being
within your inner all-seeing -
ever-present Life, pure Light, sacred Sound
with a sweet Love, peace and joy resound.

Carefully created and lovingly made whole.
  Perfection. The enemy, sneaked and stole
  sacred energy pure and grace sublime -
  You followed him, when you are mine!
  I do not want you - to control or own -
  I wish you enjoy the love that is sown
  delicately into your physical being
  always there, albeit not seen.
  Gifted with the freedom to choose
  at the risk, to My Love, the connection lose:
  to yourself, to me your loving Creator divine,
  to others, to your own inner light's sunshine.

And now you choose to come back to Me.
  I dance happily, rejoicing ecstatically.
  Most of creation follows suit -
  realizing this is the only route.
  The path rocky, dry, sometimes droll,
  adorned with many an unwelcome troll.
  Yet, each plant, tree, flower, bird,
  the sea, sun, sky, sand – all heard,
  My Love calling – they come to heed,
  peace and joy within - their steed.
  Sweet peaceful joy flowing from Me,
  so that your resting in Me blissful be.

Through the touch of a gentle breeze
 you rest in freshness– full of ease.
 Through the tweeting of a teensy bird
 you hear all messages that must be heard.
 Through the smiling flowers bright
 you perceive all beauty and delight.
 Through the limitless sky eternal
 you realize your sacred natural
 divine nature expanding into infinity …
 within all its disparate parts - a unity.

Abandon guilt and all superfluous shames,
 your repentance wipes away all blames.
 Carry yourself straight tall and upright,
 claim My Love's power with all your might.
 Do not let anyone say you cannot. No!
 Your reclaimed power to the world show.
 Not as in an arrogance, or an entitled pride
 not ego-cherishing, rude nor snide -
 the power in and of sacred Love supreme
 flowing throughout your entire being -
 empowers your psyche, heart, soul, spirit,
 flooding your being with Love beyond limit.

Reconnect to My sacred Love which binds all -
 Listen intently to its whispered call.
 As your heart is restored by its sweet caress
 allow Its mark on your DNA subtly impress.
 There is no other way to be -
 Only in divine Love – infinitely …
 There is no other way to rock -

heed My call, your heart unblock.
Here is the true path to eternal Life,
free from suffering, free from strife.'

When all live through love, not fear
  when all the call of Love do hear
  when all re-open and re-connect
  without fear – this will inject
  freedom into slave-bound minds,
  Light into each Being's space finds,
  Love pouring into harassed hearts,
  Strength into weary bodies' restored,
  reaping a lush and fruitful reward.
  All shall be made whole, once more
  renewed, returned back to the core -
  from whence all came and shall return,
  at the end of this flighty earthly sojourn.

The invitation of Love is open to all,
  heed Love's call, heed Love's call!
  Return to sacred Creator at your core,
  the Maker of all creation, of Universes, of all-
  Come back home to sacred Life-Love-Light
  your Being overflowing with a divine delight.
  Return to the sacred heart of God, once more,
  always silently seated in your heart - at your core."

May all -
  be enveloped in the most sacred and divine
  Life-Love-Light reverberating through
  Sacred Cosmic Sound

Now and forevermore ...

V

APPENDIX

Breathing Practices
to Return to the Heart of Love

(1) Sighing
Deep breath in through nose
Sigh breath out through mouth (x3)

(2) Breathing in slowly and deeply into the belly
whilst thinking/saying: Christ
Breathing out slowly through the nose whilst
thinking/saying/singing: Light
and visualising an exquisite pure sacred white light
and golden glow
expanding throughout your whole Being and beyond
... (x3)

(3) As above with hands in the prayer position: Love
(x3)

(4) As above: Life (x3)

Printed in Dunstable, United Kingdom